ROOTS IN WATER

ROOTS IN WATER
Selected and New Poems

KATHLEEN CARLTON JOHNSON

Modern History Press
Ann Arbor, MI

Library of Congress Cataloging-in-Publication Data

Names: Johnson, Kathleen Carlton, author.
Title: Roots in water : selected and new poems / Kathleen Carlton Johnson.
Other titles: Roots in water (Compilation)
Description: Ann Arbor : Modern History Press, 2025. | Summary: "Roots in Water represents the best of Kathleen Carlton Johnson's poetry from the 1990s to 2024. In this volume, she explores what it means to live in Michigan's Upper Peninsula and beyond"-- Provided by publisher.
Identifiers: LCCN 2024056239 (print) | LCCN 2024056240 (ebook) | ISBN 9781615998609 (paperback) | ISBN 9781615998616 (hardcover) | ISBN 9781615998623 (epub)
Subjects: LCSH: Michigan--Poetry. | Upper Peninsula (Mich.)--Poetry. | LCGFT: Poetry.
Classification: LCC PS3610.O3585 R66 2025 (print) | LCC PS3610.O3585 (ebook)
LC record available at https://lccn.loc.gov/2024056239
LC ebook record available at https://lccn.loc.gov/2024056240

Roots in Water: Selected and New Poems.
Copyright © 2025 by Kathleen Carlton Johnson.
All Rights Reserved.

ISBN 978-1-61599-860-9 paperback
ISBN 978-1-61599-861-6 hardcover
ISBN 978-1-61599-862-3 eBook

Cover design by Mona Z. Kraculdy
Cover image by Kathleen Carlton Johnson
Ms. Johnson's portrait courtesy of Clyde Mikkola

Published by
Modern History Press
5145 Pontiac Trail
Ann Arbor, MI 48105

www.ModernHistoryPress.com
info@ModernHistoryPress.com
Toll-free 888-761-6268

Distributed by Ingram Group (USA/CAN/AU/EU)

ROOTS IN WATER
Selected and New Poems

KATHLEEN CARLTON JOHNSON

Modern History Press
Ann Arbor, MI

Library of Congress Cataloging-in-Publication Data

Names: Johnson, Kathleen Carlton, author.
Title: Roots in water : selected and new poems / Kathleen Carlton Johnson.
Other titles: Roots in water (Compilation)
Description: Ann Arbor : Modern History Press, 2025. | Summary: "Roots in Water represents the best of Kathleen Carlton Johnson's poetry from the 1990s to 2024. In this volume, she explores what it means to live in Michigan's Upper Peninsula and beyond"-- Provided by publisher.
Identifiers: LCCN 2024056239 (print) | LCCN 2024056240 (ebook) | ISBN 9781615998609 (paperback) | ISBN 9781615998616 (hardcover) | ISBN 9781615998623 (epub)
Subjects: LCSH: Michigan--Poetry. | Upper Peninsula (Mich.)--Poetry. | LCGFT: Poetry.
Classification: LCC PS3610.O3585 R66 2025 (print) | LCC PS3610.O3585 (ebook)
LC record available at https://lccn.loc.gov/2024056239
LC ebook record available at https://lccn.loc.gov/2024056240

Roots in Water: Selected and New Poems.
Copyright © 2025 by Kathleen Carlton Johnson.
All Rights Reserved.

ISBN 978-1-61599-860-9 paperback
ISBN 978-1-61599-861-6 hardcover
ISBN 978-1-61599-862-3 eBook

Cover design by Mona Z. Kraculdy
Cover image by Kathleen Carlton Johnson
Ms. Johnson's portrait courtesy of Clyde Mikkola

Published by
Modern History Press   www.ModernHistoryPress.com
5145 Pontiac Trail   info@ModernHistoryPress.com
Ann Arbor, MI 48105   Toll-free 888-761-6268

Distributed by Ingram Group (USA/CAN/AU/EU)

For My Mother and Father
Peggy Taylor Carlton and Robert F. Carlton

Contents

Acknowledgments i

Selected Poems

Two Stones 3
Pantheon, Rome 4
The Giancolo 5
S. Maria Maggiore: Rome 6
Jesu, Rome 1996 7
Da Vinci Airport, Roma July 1996 8
American Academy: Rome 9
Notebook 10
Pronto Soccorso 11
Canticle 14
Rome Asleep 15
The Carbinieri 16
Imperia 17
Monet Spring 18
Monet's Camille at Argenteuil 19
Breakfast at Giverny 20
Paris 21
Home 22
Drama Queen Morning 23
The Sun Appears 24
Body Talk 25
Small Towns 26
Mistress of Information 27
School Days 28
River Towns 29
Sunrise, Wyoming 1958 30
La Crosse, Wisconsin 31
Nova Scotia 32
Manhattan 34
South Shore 35
Point Reyes 36
At the Beach, Dominican Republic 37
Visitor at Porta Plata 38
Utah by Air 39

On Stealing Towels from a Motel	40
Dollar Store Canned Fruit	41
Arise, Christine of Pisan	42
The End of Safety	43
Early Spring	44
Rain	45
Into Silence	46
Sunday Measure	47
July	48
Evening in Late Summer	49
Summer's Last Evening	50
Winter is Coming	51
Small Piece of Moon	52
The Real Mother Goose	53
Construction on the 101	54
Feasible Remains	55
David	56
Burying David	57
Asleep Now, No Eye Open	58
Wilma	59
Beside the Bed	60
Winter: Grand Pre	61
Morning Comes	62
Maestro	63
The Carpenter's House	64
Visiting	65
Letter to Father, at Sea	66
Hunting Season	67
Tarmo	68
Hanging Sheets	69
In Marriage, We Move so Different	70
Thrift	71
The Display	72
The River	73
Women Must Address the Body	74
The Woman Poet	75
Rocks: For Elizabeth Bishop (1913-1979)	76
The Study	77
Politics	78
Late August Aches, Knowing	79
The Execution	80
Perplexity	81

Cold Pocket 82
Wounds: For Elizabeth Bishop (1913-1979) 83
So You 84
Birthday: At Fifty 85
Love Poem 86
Please Note 87
Do You Realize 88
Three Ways to Health 89
Couple 90

New Poems

Understanding 93
The Good Wife 94
Sensitive to Gossip 95
Lament 96
Porch 97
The Farm 98
Roots in Water 99
My Father at 99 100
Nursing Home 101
Visiting Phyllis 102
Dr. Rhines of Eagle Harbor 103
Nightmare 104
A Visit from the Chaplain 105
Ceremony 106
Leaving 107

Gratitudes 108

About the Author 109

Cold Pocket 82
Wounds: For Elizabeth Bishop (1913-1979) 83
So You 84
Birthday: At Fifty 85
Love Poem 86
Please Note 87
Do You Realize 88
Three Ways to Health 89
Couple 90

New Poems

Understanding 93
The Good Wife 94
Sensitive to Gossip 95
Lament 96
Porch 97
The Farm 98
Roots in Water 99
My Father at 99 100
Nursing Home 101
Visiting Phyllis 102
Dr. Rhines of Eagle Harbor 103
Nightmare 104
A Visit from the Chaplain 105
Ceremony 106
Leaving 107

Gratitudes 108

About the Author 109

Acknowledgments

The previously published poems in this volume came from these chapbooks:

Cold Pocket (1997)
Emotional Light (1998)
Privilege of Place (2003)
Feasible Remains (2003)
Pencil Sun (2004)
Wisdom of Distance (2008)
Atlantic Time (2011)
Hotel Normal (2015)
Anonymous Breathing (2016)
End of Safety (2018)
Collected Goods (2019)
Rain of Stars (2022)

... Have we room
For one more folded sunset,
   still quite warm?

—Elizabeth Bishop, "Questions of Travel"

SELECTED POEMS

Two Stones

We have decided to become
two stones, side by side,
cast into the sea,
boiling downward, to the bottom
resting in silty gray.

Will we be satisfied,
drinking in the sea,
the sun somewhere above?

What shall we say,
nestled in each other's arms?
With water so fragile and tender,
can we endure the salt?

Pantheon, Rome

How the light drags itself round
The covered circle roof
The dome that is half apple, half heart
In the center reminding
That we are all portable,
Sitting on cold glass benches
Beneath the eye that blinks
Every 2000 years.

The Giancolo

Rome rests in a valley
A historical basin
Washed by generations.

The evening is setting
A cool breeze moving the leaves
Over the Giancolo,
The lovers line up on the walls
Kissing, the kisses of youth
The kisses of always,
Unseeing the eyes
That admire the passion
But maturely pass it by.

The veil of haze is lifting
The hills become more available
Showing towns
And low caught clouds
In the valleys preceding the city.

For all the arches and pontifical crowns
Marble and red tiled roofs,
Rome is a people
Whose eyes, whose taste,
Whose interest and disinterest
Cloud this city.

S. Maria Maggiore: Rome

A Fat Monday of sulfurous yellow vexed with incense
The exhaust of cars. Wading through the filtered sunlight
Two carpeted priests hurry across the stream of traffic.
Inside the tunnel church
The Virgin soft sitting in her painted wood,
Eyes pierced with heaven and pastel angels
She comforts with Intercession
Even those who sell religious trinkets on the venerable steps.
They are all her children, and she sews and saves
Into the blue afternoon amidst the plastic gold
And pooled intentions of the faithful.

Jesu, Rome 1996

Half a dozen prayer people
With massive missals
Men looking like movie extras,
Took up the collection
Women dusted in the light
Of commercial fixtures
Lost in prayer, for the lost.
To the left, enshrined in Baroque box
Ablaze with small cherubs and pointed rays.
The tomb of Ignatius of Loyola.
Was this a solid piece of history?
Was Ignatius asleep
Above the clatter of bus and vehicle transportation
On this hot Roman afternoon.
schools, universities, complaints,
Accusations, popes singing documents,
Limiting territory, china,
South American missions, scientist,
Reference after reference.
No this was not Ignatius,
Not resting in this little box on legs.
He was somewhere else.

Da Vinci Airport, Roma July 1996

Sitting in a leather seat,
It is two in the morning
The television is blaring
Entertaining those who wait.

The Carbinieri have already checked passports
Perhaps there is a problem
Perhaps this is normal procedure.
The hour bends the head
And I sleep amidst the luggage
My belongings holding me
Like the Arab women, to my left
With two small sons.

Awakened by music
The television has Leonard Bernstein
Giving a lecture in a tight black suit,
Aaron Copland is conducting *Appalachian Spring*,
Both men are now dead.
In Rome, they are still on the television.

American Academy: Rome

In my Armada year
Collecting perfumed evenings in ends of pink
Poems made of disk sun, sky solid
Ripe yellow pears glistening orange apricots,
A simple hallway of private doors with matching beds
Silence like cloth spread over the marble floor
The cortile fountain falling water in folds
Unending sounds, formal, continuous.

Rome, copied between thick notebook covers,
A willing transport of width and length, numbered, etched by hand,
Human measurements, building a sepulcher
To lay down the body of the lasting.

Notebook

Silverware of titles,
a collection the length of a bird's tail
same day questions nesting.
A golden apple lunch.
Sliced, served in ample silence.
Hot broth cooled on a white page.
Resting between two sheepish covers,
positioned next,
to a ruthless pen.

Pronto Soccorso

    1

The Italians are interested
In what I am doing (sketching)
But they want to look natural
So they sit by me and glance
Glance and smile.

    2

Cars go by like insects, zooming
They only have two speeds
Very fast or stopped
There is no in-between.

    3

In this city
Sound is like breathing
Only much louder.

    4

The exhaust and stream of cars
Is controlled by traffic lights
Red and green
Encouraging the citizens
To take them seriously.

    5

The window stands independent of the wall
It is the eye to the head of the house

It shuts with a green lid
Carries out the wish of owners
To make the sun important or
To close the noise out.

   6

At the Fountain of Trevi
A colorful collection of tourists
Taking obvious joy, in pulling out a coin
And throwing it over their shoulder
Not minding the cost
Rome has become a bargain.

   7

It is hot
An oppressive afternoon
The Romans gather around the Acqua Paola
To hear the water
Fall from marble lips worn smooth.

The children must touch the water
To see if it is wet
Parents nod approvingly
They want them to be Romans, always.

   8

Maria Montessori and I have been living together.
For two weeks, her face stuffed in my purse
I have bought water, stamps, tomatoes and salad
She has been with me on all my bus trips.

I have only known her as teacher
Now she is the mother of Lira.

9

Some old men approach from a portico
With what seems like a permanent smile, proud as their pin of Italy
In their lapel.

Small men in sturdy blue suits
Some with medals hanging from dipping pockets
With military accomplishments

They stand and talk,
They clap each other on the back
Whirl their arms and hands to articulate, perhaps:
Resentment, outrage or occlusion
They disappear into some secret corridor of the Capitoline
Away from the women,
Away from the tourists with cameras.

Canticle

Steel eye
climbing clematis morning
correctness of day path
symbol of unity
coming of Godhead
natural high house
permanent science
global center
separator of stars
historical absolute
certainty of Galileo
basket of morning
noon sprout glory
evening purple door
slow sinking into west
universal speaker pulling
the spent day box
    closed.

Rome Asleep

Wetting her lips with the fountain's excess
She counts the lights and makes pools glow
Retraces the ancient teeth
Exposing her historical craters to the dark
Where the mystery begins.

Rome in her nightdress, nothing supporting
The traffic flows to an ease by evening and dwindles to a cab
Night rolls in her bed, cools in silence
Bridges across the Tiber holds islands in their sleep.

In the morning tourists will return,
Fresh from hotel showers, packed in buses
That hum like arrows around cars parked
On edges of space.

The Carbinieri

A Fiat pulled up
Within two inches of my knee
Insisting on French as our language
They said I was fine
A gun slung over the shoulder
A flack jacket protecting his chest
Wearing designer eyewear, a soldier of the people.
Dressed in blue pants two red stripes
Running down the sides of his legs
His cap a crest of silver
A ball with the sun on fire
He removed this often,
To keep the sweat from rolling in his eyes.

Imperia

There is hope on the Mediterranean,
It was here that I bathed
    Buoyed by salty waves
Forcing the scatter of history
Between my lips and limps
Causing me to catch
With my salted eyes.
The mythic heroes rising
from the liquid bed.
Freeing me at last
From the anguish of being plain.

The heat, infection of the sun
Boiled like a pot
Winding its way
Into a permanent orange house,
Here I stayed inside the bluest breath on earth
a curious product
Shining as the walls holding
    The sea.

Monet Spring

A drift of cloud in streams of south wind
Branches, calling the face,
Solid green, bent by shadow
The natural force visible on the pond
Blue greens edging the water's lips.
Tall plants shelter in tongues the obscure violet dressing
What Monet left, at Giverny, is all that blue.
Hung out to dry its pale reflection, canvassed
Dipped in pure natural light.

Monet's Camille at Argenteuil

Wearing a red kimono, in the morning
and the night till he makes a church
out of her small slathers of pink.
Her whole body floating inside the house.
She resides where she has been led,
where Monet looks for a point of entry
to regain confidence, true, for he was master
of love as well with poor posture
and extra weight like layers of paint.

Breakfast at Giverny

Camille with childish fiery eyes
is a drift of cloud in streams of south wind,
branches calling to her face,
her solid green dress bent by shadow
at the kitchen stove frying pagan bacon
on a copper bottom pan.
There are blue greens edging her lips,
tall plants shelter in the tongues
of her body, the obscure violet eyelashes.
What Monet left of her after the bed
comes on the blue plate she serves him
in the yellow dining room,
the one marked by the cool slender green vases.
Claude dips in pure natural light
all that blue of his affection
     hung out to dry with pale reflections.

Paris

I want to know Paris
In the cold far from clogged buses
Cameras, teenage girls with earphones
The crush of cars, the lack of facilities

I want to know her in the cool of the earth
In its white sulfur, the stones of palaces
Free from tickets that allow the historical view.

I want to know Paris on her day off.

Home

I have become foreign, again
The pictures in the room I write
The chair worn to a soft pale green,
By the desk, its white oak legs stark
The shadowed wall glaring the sacred heads
Of parents, immobile,
As a funerary terra cotta.

New snow falls outside
Rounds the angular world
Slips objects into a white cover.
Silence collects the dark.

What do we call this pull, to new geography?
Where when we sleep, home is no longer
On the walls reassuring with familiar faces
Or chairs sitting meals cooked
Dishes washed in the soft light
    Of comfortable.

Drama Queen Morning

Simple beating clear voice
Chain smoking dawn ascends
Sunrise glowing in heavy cream
Sounds each tone with its own skill level,
She rides the morning pony
    Out to pasture.

The Sun Appears

Life thickened to
Natural light.
Sky says,
Mothers are not people
But galaxies of unrepeated stars
Where children, minor planets
Rotate.

Body Talk

elbows, in the front pew
my mothers, the hair curled
pink face of the child plumpness.
short hair, trimmed
sober clothing ironed
a small linear trim along the seam.
bodies talk,
recognizing ancestors,
born miles apart.

Small Towns

Small towns populated by loyalties
Never missing a chance to attend
High school football on Saturday
And pancake breakfasts held for a good cause
a place of the glowing average.

Here, sin is exotic, savored
Incidents live on forever,
a comfort that has no end.
It's a win or loses landscape
Complete with treasured narrative,

each corner surrenders its particular
to become everyday
neighbors of no particular race,
Other than the local.
They declare the earth is flat,
and believe it,
     reverently.

Mistress of Information

My education
awash in competition
all roads leading to the library,
where Miss T resided with her books,
shelved according to category
rotating magazines to newer versions
processing lists of timely loans.

Her penny loafer/cardigan style
mistaken by other students as plainness
and repetition in manner
was calculated management
teetering between exquisite balance of
citizenship, deportment, and ladylike behavior.
A Caribbean spirit
had defused its natural self
years before in exotic Bermuda
holidays of skilled entertainment.
Long narratives that always contained lost luggage, slender waists
and demure poses from a bar stool.

Ages had passed since Mother had seen to it
that lively memories of island affection were exchanged
for virginal books, all in correct Dewey order.
She was pressed into a private school
teaching Grammar,
the sticky stuff of sentences.

It was my first sway into her realm,
dressed in a blue blazer,
with the imprint of the school's crest
in the same spot where my heartbeat
close to my chest.
Education, I was learning,
was perfect attendance
and achievement inscribed
on a bronze auditorium plaque.

School Days

A gift from my mother:
Resizing the world
was a process of acquiring
language created with an eye.
The "gate" was "portal"
My teacher was annoyed
by my phonics selection.
She stood at her desk,
rigid as a wall,
demanding the comfort of obedience.
"Line up," she said, and then:
"Hold hands.
Hold hands, children!"
We marched across
the moving street,
in silence paired as
store-bought carton eggs.
I kept the portal open,
learning how to close
the gate behind.

River Towns

Picture here the air between river and the bend
overgrown banks holding back history of
Natives, French of course, the English
survived it all, then came Norwegians,
Swedes, a hardy life took the land
made it grow corn for as far as the eye can see.

This place about grain elevators
massive trucks that take the grain in and out
or the barges, that push grain up the river
little towns with Methodist churches
and Presbyterian founders.
Libraries have their sculpted images,
fearsome men with billy-goat beards
not much here about the wife or children
surely they must have added something.

This place of the car dealers on the outskirts
and shoemakers, boot makers
some married became rich
Moving to the big city for culture
Not needing boots for work.

a responsible place, of hospitals and schools
No one is hungry, no one goes without concern
they manage to live lives buying things in stores
and operating social activities,
where they participate as if at church.

These small little river towns on the Mississippi
Flow and rearrange their banks with each generation.
Retrieving from the geography what they could not
Learn in books.

Sunrise, Wyoming 1958

I am ten years old.
Traveling in a white and gray station wagon.
We are headed East.
Dawn is waking
Dark slipping to the edge of west
Melon-colored bluffs
Reach down into place
Filled with sagebrush and stumps
No trees.
We travel down a black macadam road
A thick yellow stripe dividing.
As far as the eye can see, no cars.
My father drives with automatic attention.
The car travels in basic silence
Sun lights casting a thick pattern
Of light and darks.
My two sisters are asleep in the back
mother rests on her coat,
stuffed between her head and the window,
Day reaching forward, entering distance.
The bluffs turning soft violet.
The sky washes itself in sparse Wyoming blue.

La Crosse, Wisconsin

A clean bend in the Mississippi
A genuine place tuned to manual labor,
    practical beneath the greeting,

Houses stretching one street to another
Like domesticated farm animals
Made to line up on pleasant lawns.

In the middle of town, a brewery
Boasting statistics on the cooling tanks
How many six packs per person in the world
Are in the gray stainless steel drums.

Nova Scotia
From Kingsport

I

Days cool grayed land
Vested in gold apple pockets
Orange and red feet, soft with harvest
The valley yields its heart crop.

II

Fatted east slowly rolling
In a long green snake cloud
The Blomidon rises like wheat to the West
The Minas Basin filled with heavy water
Wets its breath in the humid air
Turning a brown face away from the dotted towns

III

Across the basin a thumb of rock
Sticking straight up
Blue water in love with its irregular coast
Stars and moon watch the unruly child
Waiting springs favored status
Dung, seed, earth, the trinity
A man made religion on the land

IV

Dark Hills rising, the sun demands sleep,
Black night has its own sparkle, in the Maritime house
The night fish catch with tongue
Passion red as flowers

For the land, moving past the boat
Retreating into apples.

    V

Green harvest House
Set in the stomach of the sea
The purple red basin, wet with moon call
Stones wedged in shelves
Physical evidence of a round earth
Green packs of bladder plant
A tangled black stew, salted as memory
Of the tide left sponge floor.

    VI

The ceremony of water
Waiting the moon's command
Unfills the basin washing the land
Refills the ocean for the bobbing boats
Who ride the fish hour and safety home.

Manhattan

Pulsation ballet of leather briefs
Suit swarmed pavements, summer in Manhattan,
The emphasis here is on capital gains
Desire, it seems, must have an
Italian first and last name for style.

The buildings dwarf, lean disregarding
The flow of secretaries hastening to their desks.,
Syncopation of genders to eateries
How many salad bars and coffee shops
Can one city use? Teeth devouring wraps and sandwiches
Rice mixed with okra, shrimp with tofu.
Energy extracted as a panacea for stress,

The subway station is urine and metal
Garnished in a week of colorful advertisements.
Waits to devour those who cannot pay
    For taxis and limousines.

Here you cannot stop and cry
Or you will lose your place in line.
You must know where you are going,
And exactly how you will get there.

South Shore

Green bodies decking
        the blue flesh of lake
meet
    the horizontal claim of
two melon cloud breasts
      asleep in the distant east.

Carpet covers small cracks
     bare cliffs
suffused with brush
     pine, rugged nettle.
the land positioned
     on the fingertips
        of a small harbor
sided with white cottages
     brown rock drifts,
       nesting in the cool water
of vibrating summer.

Point Reyes

Amid the air
    arms of waves
sucked the shore,
brown hard face
rinsing in green
around,
    gargling wind
        a juggler of damp
a great fish of wet
a round shoulder of green
    beauty
the tom-tom shore,
    wet
widening the carriage between
    shore and sea
wet
driving in a row of mist,
    wet.

At the Beach, Dominican Republic

The wife or lover,
    at least a woman
Is sitting in a white lounge chair
With a man, a lover, a husband.
He is built, tattooed, middle aged
A man not wanting to be captured
    On paper with a pen.
She sits reading
A paper novel, remote, half-naked
Closed to a world view.
There is something dangerous
About her nipples pointing left and right
As she bargains with the vendor
Sipping on a plastic cup filled with gin
A small round piece of lime at the bottom.

Visitor at Porta Plata

Hearing is more than saying
in this green place of shattered light.
Long beaches bounded by cobalt seas.
land of the swimsuit,
souvenir vendor, heated sands.

I can see you in that cold place,
working at your desk, next to a sunny window.
Your civil self, dedicated to chilly studies.
You are here, wall to wall in Puerto Plata,
amidst the strong split shadows,
tiled halls and all inclusive drinks.
You come between sounds of megaphones,
Noisy rapid-fire Spanish
Both hurled into the tropical evening:
adventure here never stops,
except in the very early morning,
when the birds sing
and the wind bends the palms.

Utah by Air

Stretched below
unfriendly skin,
    terminal deserts
mountain coats,
snow caught in bed sores,
    moon hard
piles of rock lint
occasioned by red patches,
part
    of an old dog's tricks.

On Stealing Towels from a Motel

Rolling white
towels with a blue stripe
bunching them into
the luggage
the light filters through the blinds
the room filled with facial pink
natural white and
stranded yellows
watch.

The towels are walking
the bill paid,
a satisfaction smiles
keeping me well
behind the rolling cart.

It is wrong
even now
on washing days,
the electric cloth
cannot remain hidden
and only lately
caused trouble
to remind
that crime
and punishment
interfere
with love and life
and family outings
where a pool is
     available.

Dollar Store Canned Fruit

Arranged on shelves
Apricots from South Africa
Red Peppers from Peru
Canned nuts from China
Soup in a stunning red can from Egypt
    World travel for the poor.

Arise, Christine of Pisan

Claim your winnings,
a solid platform of female tongues
    women as beach blankets
rolled out on academic sand
bathe in sunny knowledge
when the sun goes down
they wend home
to bathing babies
feeding husbands or
breakfast cereal mornings,
eaten alone, with cats.
How many coats do women wear?
What seasons
gathered in the bloom?

The End of Safety

something has shackled protection
unstable gods roam
to do temporary justice
slow, dusty wisdom
hidden in odd menus
sleeps with truth,
bedmates in this solemn conflict,
yielding to some future,
victory in,
their mysterious dress.

Early Spring

Rising from branches tips
tongues unfurl
fanning the new moons path
Every grass blade natural prayer
Every window living open
      moist as birth
Fear shadows,
winter may return,
kingly, occupying with hard white hands.
Warm earth
skin, scattered, sun direct
knocks so hard
to enter.

Rain

Rain, shadow of pointed water
Sun excluded,
Rain lives in thin hours
Tempting measures to collect,
What they cannot own.

Into Silence

Fruit trees grow
    in abundance
and morning comes as gift,
evening is swifter and
    more fragile
than a moon smile,
with six-sided stars
    to populate the black.

I would steep as tea
brewed in long hours, a stone face
holding two curly eyebrows,
setting a simple table
with purple iris and trembling soup.

Sunday Measure

The sun is not screaming down heat.
The air, papery stopped,
Leaves are dented color,
Hang dutifully
        Still.

Sunday has that blank look test,
Unfolding before the unmade bed
The simple breakfast on a
Porcelain white plate.

Resting in a sea green chair,
Effortlessly thinking,
Some unconnected privacy,
Sipping the movable cup of
      Mid-morning.

July

July infested sun
Heat liquid on the morning road,
Pesky sounds of birds, isolated in air.
Stillness waiting early morning matrons, children
Mosquitoes, buckets that swing from belts
The armed locals come, plant their extra containers
in boxes, green mesh cubes,
green paper blocks, determined.

It is July, the month of steam and swimming
docks filled with fish scales and life preservers,
boats, brackish water, filling the bottom
of hulls, thundershower afternoon filled,
heat humming insects.

Don't overthink the happy moment
of instant breeze.
trapped, the sheer joy of approaching evening,
a quick dip before dinner,
sleeping between fresh air dried sheets.
Berries cooked in glass jars, on the cupboard,
Preserved.

Evening in Late Summer

It happens in summer sometimes,
stillness where the clouds like bread
for ducks have been thrown
on the sky; perfection suspending
us in the universal pond
where small fish watch
a humid moon, riding in the clouds,
rising in thunderheads to the west.

Trees are breath between bodies
pressing hollow bark,
dark brown and gray as an owl.
We have forgotten, though, winter ice
or prison rains that ruin seed.
We have traveled far to see
and wonder if outrage is still
appropriate for slaughter,
as we click our tongues
at a slit earth, root packed,
headed for darkness.

Summer's Last Evening

Summer is over when the boat
is bedded on the shore.
the last cruise, sliced water
the color of sky.
a calm, mirror world
on both sides of lake.

Water, cut by the bow allowed ripples to radiate
and then with speed, plumed wet.
water dark, fast, silver perpendicular weeds
far away and then close.
a shimmering, comb of stars.

Winter is Coming

Winter is coming
The leaves off the trees
Ground brown with wet
The circle about to turn,

Winter arriving,
Naked,
Cold,
Anonymous breathing

Small Piece of Moon

Small piece of moon
Looks down from its black bed.
Stars prick sideways
Pushing midnight around
The curve of bed.

The Real Mother Goose

Gathered the road to herself
Pleasure bent around daily practice
Taken back by promises
Of governments with unkind borders
A long journey down cool streams
To say nothing of tropical Florida,
       Where she lived.

Traveled in a pristine white car
With a parrot
Who spoke not a word
To strangers.

Construction on the 101

The flagman calls an authoritative halt
To morning travel
The road is swarmed by cautionary cones,
Looming machinery energized
Loading an entire hector of Nova Scotian stone.

We wait, as we can do no other, kept in lines
Associated with future pavement,
There is the casual sense of being measured,
A void develops, coffee sipped,
We are Biblical sheep and goats before the flagman's rod
Emptied by the space accounted for, as progress.

Feasible Remains

Driving through New England
Framed houses practical additions
Generations accommodated
In a side-field shirt town
Graveyard Yankees in bed
Their survivors of that peculiar practical speech
Attend academies peering the yellow hills
Living the privilege.

Commercial truckers, motorist pass,
The rectangular clapboard, quaint red brick
Worn by balancing, utility with trade.

David

Tunnel mouth
Open to essentials
End comes when
The images stop
Fall lightly in the
Green cubical room
The silent rebirth
    Enters quietly,
And you
    Failing to say good bye.

Burying David

Hanging,
pines embraced the quiet.
Like clean linen,
the feeling of all is well.

A county cemetery
remembering, the homemade
dolls, pinwheels, plastic flowers,
wreaths bought at Walmart
to mark care.

The undertaker arrived with
David in a small box, his name
written in black marker on the top.
After two years,
a bed to rest.

Afternoon sun shone
and made those attending,
more human than kind.

Asleep Now, No Eye Open

The last item cleaned from your dresser, a pair of
aging gloves, a wedding memento,
shoved in a plastic bag for protection,
I am unsure why things follow us after death,
collection of blouses, pants, dresses
shoes wait judgment to be kept or to discard.
    closets filled with you.
Little pieces of paper, with the words "Keep"
written in pencil, amidst scarves,
bags of pennies, nickels and quarters,
what do I do with this stack of faded concern?
How do I take the emotion out
of the rings and jewelry left?
Being as brief as I can,
stuffing black plastic bags,
trying to quiet the chatter left behind.
I am the oldest daughter inquisition,
rending verdict after verdict.
You are guilty mother,
    guilty of being human.
After this major cleansing,
you emerge, the one who wore white underwear,
and cotton nighties.
Beauty crafted from multiple jars,
face powder from England.
Anglo-Saxon pink, like the Queens.
Stashed in every drawer, a holy card,
medals, and rosaries amidst Chanel bottles,
too beautiful and classic to throw away.

Wilma

Wilma reclined in a
institutional nursing home bed.
A sparkle of past ghosted,
she was dying.
smooth hair, smooth skin,
long fingers and a short smile,
a mouth made for lipstick.

How often do we meet those
advancing into a direction
chosen by herself, for herself.
no children to bother, or husband
to call her back to a small house
with potholders and café curtains.
She was going home
knowing all along, where.

Early on a gray morning
no sun yet and
first snow setting down its direct white,
she did just that.
Let go with a telltale smile.

Beside the Bed

Night has taken the wind to bed
Made the leaves lie down
Turned out the lights except for the moon.

Like a table cleared, cleaned of chore
Dishes back in their white cupboard
Plates sitting patient with plates
Bowls nest inside the other
Forks and spoons inside their wells.

Good night,
To the post and lantern in the street
To the sun that burns away the day
To the laughing passages that we teach.

Good night,
To the stand that holds the book
To the glass that holds the water
To the bed that holds the body.

Good night,
To the air that surrounds the bed
To the softness of the sheets that cling
To the wool of the blankets that warm.

To the pillow that holds the face
The wind is hushed and moon
Blinks its whiteness
Now the call of dreams.

Winter: Grand Pre

Tangled trees
Atop the smooth black hill.
Ice glazed light menacing as knives.

Apple towns entwined
Asleep on budded arms
Sun gnaws, snow melts
Trickles a thin water
Filling the cold basin

The sea enters the eyes at the corners
Horizontal hush returning the wind
The white body loved by the long white land.

Morning Comes

Morning comes oblong
Garden stepping
Late summer of wilting vines
Setting in elastic blue
Fence kept Swiss Chard, cabbages
    Brussels sprouts
Earth claimed mold
Wet gray remains,
    Of natural death.

Maestro

From the door of the Laundromat
I recognized him.
He was looking for change
so he could reset the dryer.

His body was smooth
slowly aging in its tight
    avocado green shirt.
Two nipples perked
like a pubescent 13 year old girl.

A smooth dimpled face,
of polished skin,
the type that needs cream at night
his two washed-out green eyes lit,
he proceeded to fold his
navy blue jockeys with the silver stripe,
and a green knit mock turtleneck,
that wrestled with a yellow sweater
    drawn together by magnetic force.

His demeanor was different
not the master of the Kantele,
he was doing laundry
    colleting his wash
in the hot detergent smell of place,
    his center of the universe.

The Carpenter's House

The woodwork
soft pooled in arresting panels
sweet smile of health
an exhibit of patience
    with window seats,
a secular church,
    bathed in the north light.

Visiting

The sky is overcast
It matches the carpeting at the nursing home
My aunt is in room 113
Separated by a sheet
That hangs in bleached silence

It is her birthday
I bring flowers
They look artificial in the room

She cannot talk
Her damage sinks
Into a larger quiet
Her hands are pink with useless fingers,
Her face is telling anger and confusion,
As how this happened
    Without her consent.

Letter to Father, at Sea

Are you thinking of your little house
from your bed of waves, the house,
with cathedral ceiling, a fireplace and a small mowed yard?
Do you recall the picnic
or the summer we visited your sister in Michigan
driving all night in a two-toned station wagon?
As you lean on the rail, one foot on the second row of chain links,
the sliding sea beneath your feet.
A drenching wind passes, you do not smoke,
it is silent except for constant pulse of the engines.

I write to tell you, we miss your reliable leadership,
behaving as minors, we could be more involved
but we adjust the drapes so it is private at home.
All three of your daughters are taught adoration,
the Magnolia perfuming through the front picture window,
repairs some of the damage of living in yet, another place.

Mother has not resisted with arguments,
either social or educational.
Home is home and worthy of gratitude.
We are accessories, keeping the nation safe.
loyal to your home comings, every 8 months or so.
When you arrive, when the fleet comes home,
we polish floors and make immaculate order,
we have grown to love the time we take between,
blot out the farewells, the iron ramp that holds the dock,
to the ship where you climb and salute,
asking permission to go aboard,
we are amazed at your crispy military dress,
        like the flag, proud.

We light a candle for your protection and return, Father,
so you may resume activities
        in the home you have provided.

Hunting Season

He will appear, after work
going straight to the closet,
pull out a satchel and stuff it,
underwear, socks, pants and shirt.
In a plastic bag, toothbrush, paste and comb.
So focused he cannot speak.

I look as he enters the hall,
the light is dim, but it does not hide,
that distance growing between us.

The walls look geometric
cold in the shadows, his gear waits,
he rummages for his gun downstairs.

What is this that draws him into a wooded place,
to hunt and sleep amongst other males.
The primitive becomes evident.

Our homely exchanges rotate
around groceries, socks, and misplaced hats.
There is only one direction
and that is urgent.
The mandatory kiss
and he never looks back.

I have lost the person I love to a wolf's heart,
but say nothing, as expected of the wife.
For two weeks our lives stop,
sadness and sinking rotate in awkward waves.

When he returns, smelling of woodstove,
bacon grease, and sweat.
When he has showered and melted back into
the family, he will be happy,
greeting me as his wife,
and we will continue.

Tarmo

In the wind
Behind the shed
He held his hand
Blood oozed between,
His fingers, marking the snow.

He would not tell the others
He should have been more careful

If he washed it off in the barn
And made a clean bandage
No one would notice
No one would ask
How he had not taken
The sharp knife
Into account.

Hanging Sheets

Brilliant sun appointed
crisp clean two white squares
pulled sails in place,
flag snapping blanks,
forward craft between two poles,
narrowly missing collision
      with the wet earth.

In Marriage, We Move so Different

Appointments,
a drive to the dentist,
the grocery store task.
Common satisfaction
making union work.

We don't drag major issues out before dinner.
Just get the carrots out of the frig,
potatoes from the pantry
a large pot and brown the onions.
News at 6.
Eating has become the time we spend together.
the benevolence of knife and fork.
Duty so singular in its intent.
supper makes it certain,
how alien I have become.
Sitting in a chair to eat dinner,
balanced on a plate.

Thrift

No thrift in love,
no bargains,
lots of waste.
This is the gift,
to own nothing but
another dish of day.

The Display

A collection
of ancient people
stored for rarity and protection
just to the left,
on the second shelf
a pre-Columbian vase
where deer run 'round and 'round
in the vast swelling
of the middle ground,
pursued by the eternal hunter.

A primitive hymn
drenched to the skin
with sadness.

They have all learned
    to breathe,
under the water
    of the museum glass.

The River

If it is just about water
I could answer the question.
The floating and rapid
growth of pools after rain
or the mud that blackens the hull
as we pull to the shore.

Rivers, however, are usually
sandy bottomed, silt lined
stone filled with random fish.

It is the stories a river tells
between the banks,
river bends, sand bars,
the occasional sunken log,
boys jumping to swim,
merchandise going to market.

Water crossed by a bridge
must now take sides.

The river becomes political.

Women Must Address the Body

We express desire
By addressing the skin

Our discourse is with limitations
Commencing

The Woman Poet

Does the daily
    frustration
of domestic life
get inside the word
    contaminating the art.

Are there such things
as boy poems and girl poems
man or woman poems
or phallus and breast poems
poems in skirts
    or pants.

With poetry
you can build
and report the fire
all at the same time.

Appendages
make us worry
    question what matters,
the thought is
to clean and preen and prepare
no matter
    what we wear.

Rocks: For Elizabeth Bishop (1913-1979)

She knew all along,
rocks and poems are alike.

They are hard
pounding,
brutal work
    of the word attack.

When dropped into water
if right
       they float,
the weak
       sink.

The Study

Pools of sweet tea,
book piles,
rumpled sheets of pages
round the room, in no surprise

bits of poems
tasted,
tossed and advanced toward
disease.

between the white sheets
of spirits and the perfume touch,
whittled boats
        of words.

Politics
(Elizabeth Bishop returning to Brazil after Lota's death)

How do you all know
that a red line has been drawn
around my house.

Is someone reading my letters
at the top of their voice,
to the community.

Has some rule
made the authorities
stamp my important buildings
out of reach
and for what reason.

You blame me
for something
I had no idea
would happen,
I cannot be held responsible
for what others see as love,
and the ownership
    implied.

I sent her back to you
and now you cause
all this troubled water.

I have not changed,
I wish to live in peace.

Late August Aches, Knowing

The exchange, soon to come,
night features dart flying insects,
sound pools on screen
revives, questions not present in spring,
have we used up potential
    or only walked in rings,
have we closed persuasion?
distressing the moon, to speak
past affections worn thin.

The Execution

How am I to be chastised,
in front of the open door of my family,
the house of my Mother.
They will leave my hands and feet, bleeding
at her small gray house by the river.

My neighbors have
come out of their saffron houses
to witness,
an expectant crowd
layered with faces
I have known all my life.

It is no longer painful
it is a matter of fact,
it is too late to say I loved,
and too late for you to know
that this was so.

I have grown cold
a tower
whose shade
shelters and consoles.
the sun fills to black
and the heat of the morning will soon
    cool all silence.

See,
what is left,
a voice surrounded by air,
the remains
    of one faithful.

Perplexity

Rattling soul,
In a tin container.
The roundness of the marble,
Allows no corners to catch.
In the end
It is not about the marble at all,
    But the noise it makes,
Cutting silence down
    To a thread.

Cold Pocket

The sky and ground, wear
milk of snow,
    mounded
into piles.
White windows of
houses
standing on toenails,
sleeping like children
silent,
    firm in their beds.
Trees asleep on the children's shoulders
    eyes shut,
the morning slipping
into its
    cold pocket.

Only our thoughts,
so oddly isolated
in this landscape,
are free to come and go,
without coat or hat.

Wounds: For Elizabeth Bishop (1913-1979)

The hands of the aging poet,
white as a sheet
the unwritten words
"I thought you loved me" in Portuguese.
The suicide
left unmarked,
on the lips of Brazil.

Lota slept
into the photos
taken at Ouro Preto
Parque Do Flamengo and the studio at Samambaia
into the bags of coffee
that she brought as gifts
offerings, for New York.

Elizabeth
visiting the hospital for five days
extending her mandatory
participation,
hoping she could avoid
    forget,
the arrangements,
sending back the body
to the family
    all the explanations.

The realization
the fruited clot
raising in the northeastern throat,
like a fish bone
    ached
and gave patience
and opportunity
to contemplate
how love
    wounds poets.

So You

Shifting heart
to an afternoon place,
open the black and orange
patterned curtains,
let the sun
     sift and radiate.

Come close,
hand me the
fruit you brought,
red tinctured apples,
swelling, golden pears.
we will wash
the staleness away
with water,
and let the tone capture us,
     in our afternoon
of violet drapery.

Birthday: At Fifty

Can a Valentine
    break hearts
and never know it?

Years
       of trembling stars, a tin roof
   cautiously
worn as cloth
    to the edges of matter.

Half life's poor bitten
   frame
   a door to words
a brush to stroke.

Love Poem

Two places
    ripe,
eventually crossing.

Two candles
that follow
    as the wind blows by.

Two boats
    high at sea,
friendly in the adventure.

Two birds
telling the same tales
    about family matters.

Two revolutions
    Like rifles,
waiting to be important.

Two hearts
    swollen with long
      days apart,
heading home.

Two corpses
    beautiful and clean
wanting the same bed.

Please Note

dark sky rolled gray,
    clouds linger,
        whimpering rain.
trees in the valley
rotate between multiple leaves
and sparse bone breath.

in the heart,
not one leaf turns red
    without you.

Do You Realize

Do you realize
you are kept
in a drawer
smooth and abundant
like kisses on paper
one sheet laid upon the other
filed under
contiguous, resolute,
indelible
rifle to my heart

Three Ways to Health

1

Keep your love letters
Keep them
until you need them
and they need you.

2

A poem is just a pattern
On a page.
It comes to life
When it comes from your mouth
Through the roof of your heart.

3

To unpack living
you need
the four tined fork of passion
spoon's smooth bowl of heart
and China white plates of grace.

Couple

I see you as the salt
see me, the water

you the kind
me the rattled

compassion your pen
I scribing weakness

keep me by you
as we enter the sea

wind damaging
waves curling risk

storms pass
we can outlive distance.

NEW POEMS

Understanding

I can't worry anymore who loves me,
what pages to read, in what book,
or where to go after sleeping all day.

Life pushing into territories, like a shoe,
the foot sliding down to the toe area
the heel snug in its own end, yet,
uncomfortable with its shape.

House, wakes,
made of living
the firmer the day
the greater the root.

The Good Wife

knows where to find things;
can retrieve a white shirt,
dress shoes, and keys,
even wayward wallets.

She is a curator of documents,
addresses of relatives, marginally attached.
She tracks taxes, condiments,
lotions, and birthdays.
Can retrieve bargains at the grocery
with satisfaction.

Her clothes are managed,
including the latest styles
but always modest.
In the laundry,
where clothing collides with soap,
she folds soft piles for relocation.

Sitting in the evening
she writes to her sister,
who lives abroad,
how the work continues
in satisfying hours.

Sensitive to Gossip

She surrounded herself,
chairs, spoons, and plates.
Ordered the linens, washed the pots
attached to duty, and local talk.
Mornings create repeating,
repeated, and again.
Pleasing others arranged
for tidy intersections
between grocery and friends.

On a black dog day
she fell into bed,
aggravated by what had been said.
Pain accompanied by orange discharge.
They found her expired,
clutching a purple duster
against unseen piles of venial sins.

Lament

An odor of a rising moon
Dancing down
Penetrating night
Humid with memory

Porch

First light fisted
A tight sun
Water breathing
Perfect blue.

Trees canopy yet
Of summer
Shelter and kind
To wind
Carrying bluejays
Fast flying
Through the morning
Wind.

The Farm

Fields mowed hay brittle
covering the bald field in
a net of stalks
Evening scattered in dry lines

Wind driving the agitated hands
of branches waving timely union
of green fence, green face

I would sleep in the field
drench myself in night showers
Stars, hoard of celestial sound

Odd hours when common sleep surrounds
ceilings of rest
giving my notes a paper bed
the private wealth of text

Roots in Water

Mother bush
trusted stem
freed by a snip
in a pickle jar
submerged in
clean water.

Welcome collects
along with sun
urges small
fingers for
a white
hydrangea.

My Father at 99

Slow eating,
a finger moving over the plate,
grasping the slice of orange,
motoring it to his mouth,
a triumph starched morning,
orange drill of breakfast,
exposing one more day.

Nursing Home

Around the bed
isolated drug stillness
Afternoon collides with evening
Lunch, mistaken for dinner
The room has a blue door
A magnet nameplate
so it can be moved easily

The room holds two
Divided equal territory
Photos of crochet crosses,
photos of grandchildren
All nest in rectangular frames
All fading from direct sunlight
a wedding photo
The before and after
of human attention

At night
when the pain gets excessive
she will call the nurse on duty
Tell her she is thirsty
The nurse will bring a large
red plastic cup, filled with water

This is not what she wants,
not what she wants at all

Visiting Phyllis

With that smile
of a third-grade teacher,
she sparkled at the chance
of a visit.

She sits up.
Congestion is certain;
the disease is terminal,
but the human need to greet

a coveted guest is stronger.
Dying takes lots of property.
You may miss the crescendo
if you leave the room for lunch.

Dr. Rhines of Eagle Harbor

Always part of my summer
Born in Kearsarge on the copper route
Slim and plain, she walked everywhere.
Visited our small cottage with conviction.
Her voice serious with observations,
no gloss, no gossip.
Born into a doctor's household
Education focused on neuroscience.
Graduation from Northwestern
Teaching at the University of Chicago.
Research in laboratories testing, writing results
Honors and advancement,
She stood by herself.

In the summers, when she came to the Harbor
She would encourage me
As a girl to think and explore
As a woman, she passed around courage,
Advancing, always advancing.

What is it about funerals,
sweeping the person up
buried in a pine cemetery
asleep under name and dates?
A light burning,
for those who know,
where to look.

Nightmare

Fastened eyes closed,
My body suffers float in
Dark menacing
Acid in the back
Of my sleeping mouth.

A Visit from the Chaplain

A green, sea foam house
with an ordinary porch.
Inside a man connected by hoses.

You may talk about your living God
but Death manages a presence,
a long shadow greedy for space.

In the dark living room,
smelling for animals.
The patient sits on
a faux leather recliner.
He is vulnerable but refuses help.
The wife sits across on a kitchen chair.
She cannot help, only advise.

We draw to completion,
setting a date for the next visit,
a formality for next week,
call before coming.

I leave down the porch steps,
clutching my zipper-cased Bible
in my right hand,
breathing in the crisp clean air
of late March.

Ceremony

As the seasons turn
one to the next, so we travel
from East to West.
We rise and flow with the years.

In summer we gather sun
green earth.
In winter the cold
that coats us with snow.

Walking in the shadows of those
who has gone before,
we imagine the many to come,
we are afloat in a pool of people.

The ocean continues with waves.
The sky with white clouds
and the moon at night
makes its rounds.
Sun shines a trusting face daily.

May you sleep in hope,
rest in peace,
may love gently keep you
in its care.

Leaving

In the old days
I would have been allowed
a bit of bread and a blanket.
We do not think like that anymore.

A journey widens the eye
we have crossed and heard in loud terms
futures assigned.

but the wooly branches
and naked fingers say nothing.
Winter is coming, they remain still.

The valley full of stone markers
roadways pointing so clearly.
Home, banisters of oak and ash.
A wood house carved from minimum.

The light fades to the hill, cool stars wake
while over the valley floor
edges wander to harsh pink of sky.
Items take shapes of small packets
and books tucked between layers of wool.

I know before I start,
there will be loss.

Gratitudes

I want to thank Raymond Luczak for his editorial skills and the Upper Peninsula Publishers and Authors Association (UPPAA) for giving me many opportunities and encouragement to get this book out. Also a special thanks go to Deborah K. Frontiera, who got me into the group in the first place. Otherwise, these words would have sat in multiple chapbooks and notebooks there to languish without light.

I am thankful for the beautiful vistas and geography of Maritime Canada and the trips made to Eagle Harbor as a child. The crossings of Wyoming one fall. New Orleans for its glitter and bohemian dress. Virginia in its colonial history and Arlington, where my grandfather took me to lunch at the National Art Gallery. For a beautiful trip to Quebec and home again with my two daughters.

I am more than grateful for the many poets whose work has enriched my life with their example and poetry. The list is endless, starting with Elizabeth Bishop, Czesław Miłosz, Tomas Tranströmer, Mary Oliver, and May Swenson.

About the Author

Kathleen Carlton Johnson came from a military family and lived in various places. She received her education in Virginia at the College of William and Mary in Williamsburg and furthered her education at Villanova University and the University of Virginia. She has taught and ran libraries, but books and poetry have always been a part of her. The poems selected for this book span some 50 or so years. She has produced some 16 chapbooks. Since she's also a visual artist, poetry and painting complement each other. She is currently a Chaplain in Hospice, which has been a gift not only to her soul but to her art.

Her work and visual art have appeared in *Rattle, MacGuffin, The Diner,* and *Barely South*. She has also been published in *The Origami Poems Project, Nassau Review, William and Mary Review,* and most recently, *3rd Wednesday, U.P. Reader,* and *Yooper Poetry*.

She lives six miles from Calumet/Laurium, where she was born. With her family now grown, she is entwined with grandchildren and the beautiful Upper Peninsula of Michigan at her doorstep.